WHAT NOT TO SAY TO YOUR HUSBAND

WHAT NOT TO SAY TO YOUR HUSBAND

JASON HAZELEY & NICO TATAROWICZ
ILLUSTRATED BY SARAH SUMERAY

Quercus

First published in Great Britain in 2020 by

Quercus Editions Ltd
Carmelite House
50 Victoria Embankment
London EC4Y 0DZ

An Hachette UK company

A CIP catalogue record for this book is available
from the British Library

HB ISBN 978 1 52941 149 2
Ebook ISBN 978 1 52941 150 8

10 9 8 7 6 5 4 3 2 1

Text designed and typeset by CC Book Production
Printed and bound in Great Britain by Clays Ltd, Elcograf S.p.A.

Jason Hazeley is a comedy writer, podcaster and musician who co-authored *The Ladybird Books for Grown-Ups* series and *Cunk on Everything*. He also co-authored *Instructions for the British People During the Emergency* with Nico Tatarowicz.

Nico Tatarowicz is a comedy writer, actor, podcaster and musician, who has worked on the BAFTA-award-winning *The Armstrong & Miller Show*, *Murder in Successville*, *Crackanory*, and *Very Important People*. He co-authored *Instructions for the British People During the Emergency* with Jason Hazeley.

Things you should NEVER
say to your husband
are marked with a

What Not to Say . . .

. . . When He Hasn't Looked Up from His Phone for Three Hours

If I get in there, will you talk to me?

Have you finished Twitter yet?

Are you reading about phone addiction again?

Listen – why don't you do all your bootie calls during the day, then we can watch a movie at night?

I think it's time you started wearing a dopamine patch.

Say hello from me to everyone you've ever met.

Just to let you know: it's 2044 and I'm married to an android.

Have you joined a *Black Mirror* re-enactment society?

. . . When He's Ill in Bed

Is this you Never Getting Ill again?

Can you sign this? It's your new will.

Are you well enough to peel a load of onions for me?

```
playback NORMAL/EQ 120 HS

Date FUNERAL PLAYLIST  Noise Red._____  No.____
I hope that Something better comes along-Jim Henson
Another one bites the dust-Queen
Highway to hell - AC/DC
Stayin' alive- The Bee Gees
The Countdown theme tune (for Casket lowering)
Get on up -James Brown
Cold as ice-Foreigner
Get up, Stand up-Bob Marley
Celebration- Kool & The Gang
Friday- Rebecca Black
```

I'm just making a playlist up for your funeral.
Do you think Kylie's a bit too upbeat?

Not like you to lie around moaning.

Don't be offended, but I've booked you into a Travelodge for
tonight.

(SNIFFING THE AIR) Fuck me. Where are you hiding the
Stilton?

I can't believe you've let this happen. Again.

Thinking ahead, do you want a normal or a wicker coffin?

2

I've just been watching that film *Misery*. Have we still got that camping mallet?

You know Dermot from work? His other half's ill in bed too, so the two of us are off to the cinema tonight.

Are you going to even *try* to get better?

On your headstone, do you just want 'DIED OF A COLD'?

Just to be on the safe side, I think we ought to burn that bedding when you're better.

Look – I don't want me and the kids catching this, so we're going to Florida for a few weeks.

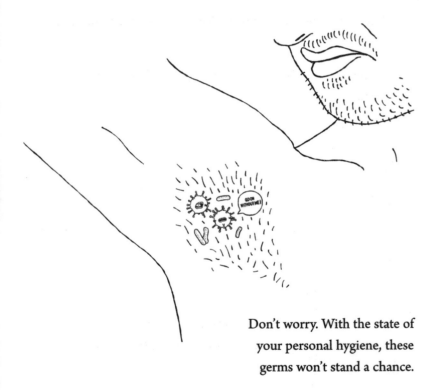

Don't worry. With the state of your personal hygiene, these germs won't stand a chance.

. . . In a Supermarket

That'll look nice in the bin in three weeks.

Don't go up the biscuit aisle. You'll only get upset.

Shall I tell the cheese counter that the ambassador's here?

There must be one of these coffees we haven't got a machine for.

Stop fidgeting. The beer's still going to be there in ten minutes.

I wish you looked at me
the way you look at those doughnuts.

Why don't you go and see if they've got any burnproof rice?

Don't stand there too long – you'll end up in the bargain bin.

Look – we'll do this quicker if we split up. And I do mean 'get a divorce'.

Oh, is Loyd Grossman cooking for us again tonight? How exciting.

Buy an extra box of tissues – I've got something to tell you later.

Crinkle-cut chips? Do you think we're made of money?

Don't bother getting a lottery ticket. I think we'd know by now if you were lucky.

Come on. Let's get away from these fridges. We don't want your dick getting any smaller.

. . . When He's Been in the Loo a While

What are you doing in there? A podcast?

... When He's Home an Hour Later than He Said He Would Be

Oh, it's you. Are you going to do your impression of a sober person?

It was so romantic of you not to hang around for the sambucas.

If this was a job, you'd have been fired a long time ago.

You're an hour late. If you're having an affair, I want to know what you were doing for the other fifty-seven minutes.

You're early. I'm usually pretending to be asleep when you get in.

The Usborne
Book of
Time-Telling
For
Drunks

Learn how
to focus
even when
wasted!

Never get
caught out
again!

I think we might have to get you the Usborne book of *Telling the Time.*

For a very special treat, can I watch you make your drunk snack?

Don't tell me – you helped an old lady cross the road 300 times.

You're back. Another dream dies.

Damn. I'd already started looking at wallpaper.

 Your timekeeping's up there with your oral sex technique.

. . . When He's Off to Robert Dyas

Remember: we need an extension cable, not a miniature Hoover with an iPhone speaker on it.

Don't be longer than six hours in there.

Should I start seeing this Robert Dyas person as a threat?

I'll phone them and warn them that you're coming again.

What more have you got to do to get a Robert Dyas black card?

Don't overdo it. There's no more room in the loft.

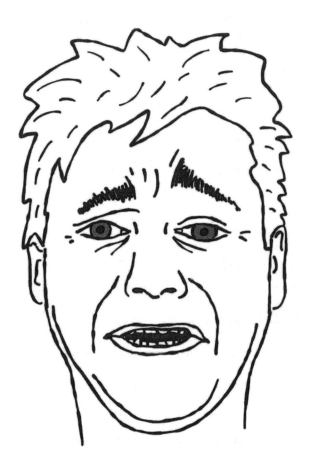

Shall we stay in tonight so you can tell me which films
are better than the one we've chosen?

. . . When You Pick Him Up from the Airport

Good job you texted me. I'd completely forgotten you.

You landed, then? Oh well.

Can't believe you got through, after all the stuff I told Interpol.

I may have hidden some dark chest hairs around the house, but it's nothing to worry about.

I hope you're not expecting sex, because I've had enough of that this week.

Nothing much has changed here. Apart from the locks.

Well, they say absence makes the heart grow fonder, so, since you're already packed, why don't you hop on another flight?

Where shall I drop you? Your mum's?

I missed you so much. For the first hour.

I know you'll have missed your stuff, so I've put it all up the drive for you.

Well, my end-of-holiday blues are kicking in. How about you?

Don't feel you have to come with me.

Don't get excited – I'm not here to pick you up. I'm a minicab driver now.

I was going to write your name on one of those boards, but I can't remember it.

Oh God. You think you look well, don't you?

I've bought you a coffee, because you've got shitloads of housework to do when you get in.

 Shame about your flight going smoothly.

... When He's Holding His Nose while Hosing the Bin Out

Come on, darling – if I can sleep with you, you can do this.

... While He's Following a Recipe

Would you like me to read out the words, darling?

Shall I book a few days off?

Have we still got that box of Diocalm?

. . . On His Birthday

Happy birthday, darling – I've booked you a consultation with a surgeon to see if he can get you to smile.

But I thought you liked the Baha Men.

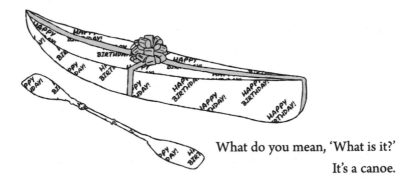

What do you mean, 'What is it?' It's a canoe.

I know you don't like me choosing you clothes, so I bought myself a new coat.

Now, don't get too excited, because I haven't bought you anything.

But I bought you a present last year. What do you want another one for?

I wanted to take you somewhere you'd really like, but I couldn't find a restaurant with a shed.

I wanted to make this year special, so I'm going to a spa.

I was going to get you clothes, but you'll only grow out of them.

. . . While He's Trying to Park the Car

You're gonna nail this one day.

Stop panicking and just PARK THE CAR.

Don't overthink it.

Listen – don't feel bad. Just remember: you're good at other things.

God, this is tense.

Don't shout, but you can go on courses to get better at this.

Try not to blink. Apparently it massively raises your chances of crashing.

What insurance have we got on this again?

You can see all these other cars, right? Just checking.

I don't know if I can handle this any more.

Wow, look how red you are. I'll take a picture.

Let's be honest, I'm the 'parking one' out of us, aren't I?

Shall we go somewhere more field-y?

Here's a thought: sponge cars. Just to save all this.

Don't panic, but there's loads of people watching you.

. . . On the First Day of a New Job

See you at lunchtime, then.

Just don't be yourself.

Have you got your joke with you?

Maybe save *some* of your opinions about Batman for day two . . .

Did you change your name like I said?

If you hate it, just remember: I had to give birth.

Have you memorised the lies on your CV?

Don't mention the settlement.

Be nice to the IT department. We don't want a repeat of 'Clairegate'.

If anyone bullies you, just laugh along – we need the money.

 If you don't like it, don't worry – you can always get a new wife.

... When He's Doing His Annual Looking-for-His-Tennis-Racquet-during-Wimbledon-Fortnight

Here we go. Are you going to be looking for your flute when The Proms are on and all?

Please don't wear all whites, darling – I'm the one who has to wash your underpants.

You playing tennis? That's like Rab C Nesbitt going to watch *Swan Lake*.

Well, I think it's marvellous that the lower orders should get a chance to have a try as well.

Do you want Deep Heat for dinner tonight?

Now don't be getting all annoyed if the posh people stare at you – they've not grown up around the likes of you.

At this rate, you'll be able to serve overarm by the time you're seventy-four.

. . . When He's Rearranging Everything in the Dishwasher Yet Again

It's like watching a chimpanzee learning shapes.

If you do this another eleven or twelve times, I'm sure you can find space for one more teaspoon.

You can have your colouring book when you've finished with that.

This is how Hitler got started.

I remember when you used to look at me like that.

Well, it's nice to see you care about something.

You're wasted round here.
You could be doing this at
Nando's.

You know it's not
Tetris, right? They don't
all fit together?

What are you trying to get out of this?

You look so serious. Are we going to die if you get this wrong?

This is like the bomb disposal scene from a Finish advert.

You think you'd have cracked this by now.

Do you think about this when we're having sex?

Admit it. You are a bit Hotpoint curious.

To think you used to do backflips in nightclubs.

. . . When You Arrive in Your Hotel Room Together

For fuck's sake. I told them to put twin beds in here.

NB TEST RESULTS
READ THIS IF YOU WANT A DIVORCE
Sorry for Stringing you along all this time. xxx

. . . While He's Getting Undressed

Do you think we could have some sort of warning system for this?

. . . When He's Making Chicken Stock Again

Well, that's £1.49 we haven't lavished on stock cubes. Can we go to Mauritius now?

Ooh, you can forget to make a risotto with this and then pour it down the drain in two weeks.

Are we to start using both sides of the toilet paper as well now?

Behold! Chicken Stock Man – the world's tightest superhero.

Look out, Knorr, there's a new sheriff in town.

That'd better not be the cat in there.

Are you trying to be better than me again? Bless.

You realise our freezer already looks like a Museum of Stock.

I know things are bad, but bin soup is taking it a bit far.

. . . When He's Running His PowerPoint Presentation Past You

You might want to put some Metallica on this so they stay awake.

Remember: if they clap slowly, that's *not* a good sign.

Check out your design skills. It'll be jumble sale posters next.

Do me a favour: never, ever go on *The Apprentice*.

This'd better have a happy ending.

Is this what you do all day?

Well, now I know why you've never had an affair at work.

Slow down a bit. Bit more. Bit slower. Actually, just stop.

This is going to ruffle a few feathers.

If you say 'going forward' one more time, I will blind you.

. . . In The Bedroom

I thought perhaps we could try some role play: do you fancy pretending to be my actual husband?

I can't sleep. Tell me why *Parklife* is an overrated album again.

Have my hands got bigger?

You should go on Tinder.
They need a laugh.

Bonzo.42
📍 15 km away

I am great at multitasking (can juggle a large combination of fruits at once) and I'm also a highly-skilled makeup artist.

I love to take frequent journeys around town in my little car, along with my 40 best mates.

Looking for someone who'd like to join me on romantic unicycle rides across the country but who can handle my tendency to fall. A Lot.

I know we said we'd leave fantasies unexplored, but do you think we could at least try a twosome?

Would it join in if I turned the heating up?

. . . Halfway round IKEA

What do you want to do first – the meatballs or the seething?

I like how far apart these two beds are.

It's hard to tell how this would look without your clothes thrown all over the floor.

This unit comes with earplugs, so I don't have to listen to you putting it together.

Calm down, Kevin McCloud, it's only a fucking shoe rack.

This is the longest walk you've had in years.

I'm just trying to imagine how these shelves would look covered in your sodding *Star Wars* figures.

You know these corner sofas? Could we get one that goes round a corner so we're not in the same room?

I'm not blaming you, but I honestly thought we'd be shopping in Heal's by now.

. . . While He's Talking to an Elderly Neighbour

Sorry. He's been drinking all morning. Come on, love. Back inside.

. . . When He's Got a Bad Back

Have we still got the warranty for you?

. . . When He's Off for a Night Out with the Lads

Just remember, if you go to a nightclub, all the girls there will think you're a minicab driver.

Don't worry about making a noise when you get back in – I won't be living here by then.

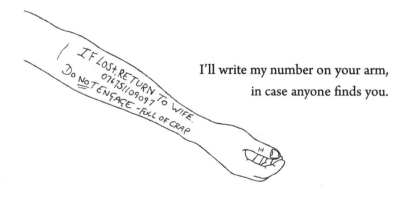

I'll write my number on your arm, in case anyone finds you.

Ooh – I think there's a vacancy in Take That.

... When He's Deliberately Watching that Programme He Hates

Is it time for your tutting exercises again?

Did he nick your dinner money off you at school or something?

Oh, I love watching your face when you really hate something.

Don't punish yourself, darling, there won't be anything left for me to do.

... When You're on the Ferry He Insisted You Take Instead of Going on Eurotunnel, Which Would Have Been Brilliant

Well, thank God we didn't spend that extra eight quid. You can buy a shit bracelet now.

Are you alright? You've gone the same colour as when I want to have sex with you.

Well, this is great. I love a prison ship that sells eau de Cologne.

I think we should do this more seldom.

At least on the *Titanic* we'd have some drama to look forward to.

I didn't expect it to be posh, but I didn't think the car park would be the nicest bit.

. . . When He's About to Spend £200 on a Chef's Knife

Is that for me?

That'll come in handy for your spaghetti on toast.

Does this mean you're going to stop eating frankfurters straight out of the jar?

. . . When He Gets His Guitar Out

I think we'd know if you were any good at this by now.

. . . When He's Trying on a Suit

Don Draper's going to shit himself.

And now it's over to Gideon with the weather.

Is there a job going in Spandau Ballet?

You're finally getting in touch with your inner rep.

People knock Asda, but you look absolutely fine.

Is that your school blazer?

Have the annual Double Glazing Awards come round again?

. . . At the Altar

So you weren't joking?

. . . While House-Hunting

Tell you what, we put a shark tank in here and this could be your evil lair.

I know it says it's an airing cupboard on the floor plan, but I reckon you could do your sulking in here.

That cat flap will have to go. I don't want you sneaking out when I'm not looking.

Just out of interest, could we buy two separate flats for this much?

... When He's in a Good Mood

You're in a good mood. How long have I got to live?

Promise me you haven't found God.

What's happened? Has KFC been nationalised?

Be careful, smiling like that. Some of those teeth haven't seen daylight in years.

Let me guess: you've won some cheese.

Are you smiling, or is it
just trapped wind?

I don't know who it is you're channelling at the moment, but tell them they can have your side of the bed.

Either that's a smile, or your piles have come back.

Have you been drinking in the shower again?

You're in a good mood. Who is she?

Don't laugh, darling. You sound like a hundred-year-old lawnmower.

Don't stay like this too long. I might start liking you again.

Your face looks different. Should I get the gas checked?

Are you actually in a good mood, or am I going to wake up in a minute?

Don't move. I'm just going to go and get my camera.

Is this going to be like *Awakenings*? Are you going to go back to your normal self in a few weeks?

You know it's not twenty years ago, don't you?

Don't panic, but I think someone nicer than you might be trying to get through.

Steady on. You don't want to sprain your cheeks.

. . . After a Haircut

OK. Let's not panic.

The bastards! Who did this? Did you get a look at them?

Finally got the bollocks to join the army, eh? Fair play.

Whoever you're trying to look like, you should phone them and apologise.

Is this your way of telling me you're joining a tribute band?

That's a bit much. Did you shout at the hairdresser or something?

What's happened here? Was there no mirror?

Aww, you let a baby cut your hair!

How many haircuts is this supposed to be?

. . . Just before You Enter Your Parents' House with Him

I might have said some sex stuff to Mum. If she brings it up, just laugh.

. . . On the Morning of a Doctor's Appointment

Ask if there's anything they can do about your mind.

. . . At the Airport

I wish you were as scared of drinking as you are of flying.

Shall we buy you a book you can hold while you look at all the totty round the pool?

Do you want to start telling me how much you hate sand now, or shall we wait till we get there?

. . . When His Friend Who Was in That Band is on His Way Over

You should play him some of your songs. The ones that sound like they're from *Balamory*.

Do you want me to fetch your cowboy boots for you?

Why don't you go and get your guitar, so he can get it out of first gear?

Mad to think: that could have been you, if you'd had any talent whatsoever.

OK, so he's toured Japan, but has he ever finished that 1,000-piece jigsaw of the Death Star?

Do you want me to hide your slippers and scatter some Jack Daniel's bottles around the place?

Talking of rock and roll, tell him about that time you had that chilli scotch egg at the farmers' market.

If you ask your friend nicely, he might let you join in at one of his concerts.

. . . When He Tries One of His Conspiracy Theories on You

Last time you had a toothache it was Mossad's fault.

I'm so glad I married someone cleverer than science.

I can't keep up with these.
Is Prince Edward still a
shape-shifting stick insect?

Thank you so much for putting all your time into researching this stuff – it makes raising the kids on my own worthwhile.

It's funny – you didn't put 'internet loon' on your dating profile.

Remind me never to meet your friends.

Well, thank God someone's finally done some proper research on YouTube.

David Icke called. He wants his shell suit back.

I read this theory on the internet that, if you go on like this, we're not going to be married any more.

. . . . When He Proudly Presents You with a Lovingly Grilled Artisan Cheese Toastie

This better not be your way of telling me you've bought a food truck.

You seem to have rescued this sandwich from a fire. Is everyone alright?

... On Valentine's Day

You know what today is? Yep. Simon Pegg's birthday.

Don't think I've forgotten Valentine's Day – I've just forgotten how to have feelings.

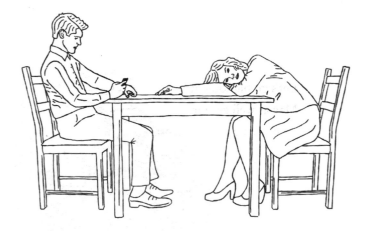

Let's do something quiet tonight,
like not speak to each other for three hours.

Don't buy me a new card – I haven't opened the one from last year yet.

I know you don't like big, romantic gestures, but I've wormed the dog.

Do you remember our first Valentine's Day? That Pad Thai was fucking sensational.

A bit awkward, this, but I'm double-booked tonight. Can you do Wednesday?

Let's go big tonight. May as well go out with a bang.

. . . When He Can't Make His Mind Up What to Choose from the Menu

You didn't take this long choosing me.

Have you got cataracts or have you just not made your mind up yet?

Before you ask, there's no such thing as Chinese sausage and mash.

You look like you're in agony. It's the chips debate again, isn't it?

Hurry up, Jay Rayner – you had a Bombay Bad Boy last week.

We should take this menu home. You could read it every time I'm watching *Love Island*.

Do you want me to help you with some of the big words?

We actually came out to eat *at the same time.*

Shall I just see you back at home?

. . . When He's Doing Movember

You should grow a personality to go with that.

. . . When He's Leaving the House Thinking He Looks Dapper

If it's anyone younger than forty-five, you're wasting your time.

Tell you what – you'd turn some heads tonight if you walked into a bingo hall.

Have you been to the jumble sale without me?

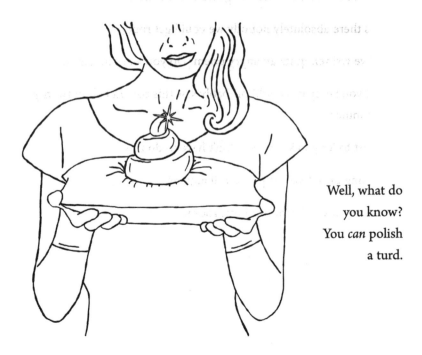

Well, what do you know? You *can* polish a turd.

. . . When It's Just the Two of You

Should have said, really, but I've written a will.

Well, this is awkward, isn't it?

Shall we try facing away from each other?

I've got a good idea: why doesn't one of us go for a walk?

Strange. I used to enjoy this.

Shall we have one last shag and call it a draw?

Is there absolutely nobody we could get round?

I've written quite an angry poem. Do you want to hear it?

If you fancy it, I could probably saw this sofa in half in twenty minutes.

Just to let you know: we don't have to do this.

Hang on – I've just got to call anyone.

Sorry, love, I've booked this room.

. . . When You See a Poster Advertising a Medium

You should go to that. See if she can put you in touch with your sense of humour.

. . . When He's Suddenly Interested in the World Cup when the Rest of the Time He Couldn't Give a Shit about Football

Ah, Professor Football. I was wondering when you were going to show up.

Oh, how sweet, you're trying to be 'blokey' again. Shall I go and get you a dirty vest and a can of Foster's?

Is this your month-long holiday from total sporting ignorance?

This is like when you started wearing a bandana because you saw Keanu Reeves do it.

Oh, you've found a new way to ignore me. Good for you, darling.

Shall I print out the offside rule for you so you can join in with your friends?

OK, you can watch it, but don't paint a flag on your face and upturn any German cars, right?

Why exactly are you doing this? Is it so you can talk to taxi drivers?

By the way, your membership card's arrived for the Performative Sports Interest Society.

What the hell's going on here? It's only a week since you were crying at *Queer Eye*.

. . . When He's Hung-Over

Good morning,
Oddbins.

L'Eau du booze

Notes of Smirnoff, JD, and generic white wine.

It's not the antibiotics – it's the beer you put on top of them.

If you're checking my face for signs of sympathy, you're still drunk.

Go and brush your teeth. It's like being breathed on by Scotland.

If you think you feel bad now, wait till you remember how rude you were to the fire brigade.

Oliver Reed's baton arrived for you this morning.

... When He Tries It On

I see you're having your idea again.

Read the room, mate.

Alright. But this is the last time.

OK, but first I just want to count *exactly* how many peas we've got left in the freezer.

Did I miss a Barry White record?

Are you Daniel Craig? No? Fuck off, then.

How long do you think you can hold that thought for?

You're not a quitter. I'll give you that.

Has our Sky Sports subscription run out or something?

☢ Don't feel you *can't* offer me money for this.

. . . When He's Deciding Which Cordless Drill to Buy

Do any of these come with a proper man?

. . . In Morrison's Car Park in the Rain

Is it raining in Morrison's car park? I hadn't noticed.

I haven't been this disappointed since our first date.

You really come alive here.

I've brought you here for a very special reason. We've run out of potatoes.

I never dreamed that this would be our life.

Listen – only a thought – but, if we stay here till midnight, we could try dogging.

This reminds me of that poem you read out at our wedding.

Kicking myself that I didn't ask you to marry me here.

Don't forget to say hello to your bottle bank.

. . . At the Wedding Reception

So, how long do you think we should stay married for?

Well, this is all a bit real.

I was only joking when I asked, but this is absolutely brilliant.

Darling, this is my solicitor.

It's funny to think this is the best you'll ever look, isn't it?

You look as handsome as my daddy.

Shall we just go home?

. . . When He's Wearing Walking Sandals

Well, they're not comfortable to *look* at.

Sorry who's this?

just went to Google sth on your laptop and it autocompleted AFFORDABLE VASECTOMY

I was thinking of kissing you when I get in, so start defrosting your face.

I really appreciate everything you do for me.

Sorry that was meant for my therapist xxx

if you can hear knocking next door don't worry it's only me

I've done some homework and sex therapists are quite expensive, so I've put on some make-up and I'm going to set off the smoke alarm

I fancy a naughty weekend away, so me and my vibrator are going to Portugal.

you just looked straight through me at the lights

Morning. Didn't want to wake you, but I've moved to San Francisco.

Send me a dick pic. I want to compare it to something.

Just passed that Italian restaurant you like. It's shut down because we NEVER GO OUT.

I'll Skype you when he's left for work SO HORNY RN

While you're at the shops, don't forget we're married.

. . . When You're Introducing Him to Someone

This is my first husband.

This is someone I married.

...When He's Watching *George Clarke's Amazing Spaces* and Making Notes

You know that these people actually made these sheds themselves, right – and it wasn't the Shed Fairies?

Aww, it's lovely seeing you get excited about a new challenging idea for nine minutes.

Hey, don't go to all that trouble – just go and live somewhere else.

Judging by the language when you painted the bedroom wall white, I might have to get my ears removed if you try something like this.

I think *Amazing Spaces* might be a bit of a stretch for you, darling. Is there a programme called *Half-Arsed Unfinished Projects* you can watch?

... When He Starts Growing His Own Veg

You do realise you're about to spend eight months building a small salad, don't you?

Good for you, darling. Shall I do a press release for the slugs?

It's amazing. You can kill herbs quicker than Sainsbury's can sell them.

Is this the death-knell for that tin of peas we've had since the height of Britpop?

What's Mother Nature ever done to you?

That's who you remind me of: the vegan Hannibal Lecter.

While you're at it, why don't you try and grow a job that pays more?

I hope those courgettes have written a will.

OK, everyone – Martin tries to be Hugh Fearnley-Whittingstall, take seventy-five. Action!

You know we've still got children to tend to, don't you?

If this is the first stage of you turning into a hippy, can we just jump to the bit where you get disillusioned with the whole scene and get a haircut and a job?

If it's alright with you, I'm going to carry on going to the supermarket.

. . . When He's Training for a Marathon

Oh good. I've always wanted to see you on a stretcher in a tin foil cloak.

Why not destroy yourself doing fuck all instead? It's more fun.

Make sure you keep a note of all the sponsorship money you'll have to give back.

If you want to fuck your knees up, just keep eating burgers like they're grapes.

How are you going to do that? Are you borrowing somebody else's legs?

If you think I'm missing *Sunday Brunch* for this, you've got another think coming.

After you've done this, do you think you could train yourself to put the milk back in the fridge?

I can sense you're nearly ready to give up, so I bought you these from the pound shop.

What's the charity? Fathers for Cheese?

If you think I'm pushing you around in a wheelchair, you can think again.

. . . On January 1st

It's nearly 11 a.m. and you haven't mentioned cutting down on your drinking this year yet. I thought it was a tradition.

Will it help this year's fitness regime if I strategically place Quality Street around the park?

Oh, come off it, mate. You can hold your breath longer than you can go without sugar.

I think 'regime' might be the wrong word. Shall we just say 'afternoon'?

Are you sure about giving up booze? I'm worried we might find out who you really are.

About this 'New You' – is he any taller?

. . . When He's in Hospital for a Routine Operation

I was going to buy you a puzzle book, but we don't want you getting a brain bleed as well.

The surgeon was so impressed with your advice that, just this once, he's going to try it your way.

I've written a eulogy for you, just in case. Do you want to hear it?

God help whoever ends up sitting next to you
in the old people's home.

Do you know what? I actually prefer it on your side of the bed. Still, not long now.

I've had a word with your consultant, and you should probably swap that novel for a book of short stories.

Right – I've written a list. Which of this stuff is good to take to the charity shop?

On the plus side, if you die, your surgeon says he'll take me to Corsica.

How are you sleeping in here? I mean, probably not as good as me . . .

I'd forgotten how many men talk to me when I go out without you.

What is it about hospitals that makes me so horny? Anyway, must dash.

Well, I guess this is it.

. . . As He Launches into His One Anecdote Yet Again

This is a really funny story the first fifty times.

Join in if you know the words.

Fuck me. I've heard this more times than 'Wonderwall'.

I love this story. I'm just popping to Canada.

... When He Comes Home with a New Kitchen Gadget

Great – I'll clear a space on the shelves in the garage for it.

... When He's Off to Book Group

I didn't know you could read.

And people actually listen to your opinions, do they?

Did you finish *The Very Hungry Caterpillar*, then?

Shame it's only one night a week. Could you join another six?

Don't do your reading face. You'll get drool all down your shirt.

Have you been hiding another brain?

Do they do colouring books?

I'm not sure these are the kind of people who are going to want to discuss Roy Keane's autobiography.

. . . When You Call Him to See Why He's Still Not Back from the Chip Shop

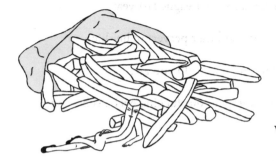

Be honest with me: are you having an affair with some chips?

You know you didn't have to catch the fish yourself?

Do you want me to come down and read the menu out to you?

Ring back twice if you've got involved in a potato siege.

Don't rush back – we've starved to death.

If you're not back in ten minutes, I'm going to eat your guitar.

Hey, listen: if you've not been served yet, come home – we've grown some potatoes.

. . . When He's Trying Too Hard with a Young Waitress

I bet she can't wait to hear your theory on why United didn't qualify for the Champions League last year.

Just what she needs: another pervert in her life.

Bless. You've forgotten how old you are.

☢ Alright, Gary Glitter, put your fucking eyeballs back in.

. . . On Date Night

You again.

Right. I'm off for my date.

. . . While He's Getting Dressed

It's probably time we thought about getting you your first bra.

. . . After He's Dented the Car

That's strange. I thought it was only women that did that.

Think of it as the car equivalent of getting a tattoo.

Did someone put a pillar in a stupid place again?

Oh, good. I was wondering how we could get our insurance up.

Did you have the satnav tuned in to Pornhub?

Bless. Were you trying to be Vin Diesel again?

Did you drive off, like we said?

You do know that if I see a missing kid in the paper, I have to phone the police . . .

. . . When He's Laying Out the Camping Equipment on the Lawn

Well, I guess this is goodbye.

Oh, you live out here now, do you? Probably for the best.

Make sure you don't forget to ask whether we like camping or not.

Shall I hide something vital now so you can be furious when we get there?

Well, that's very brave of you.
Does this mean you're not afraid
of moths any more?

This is a lot of stuff to get into a hotel room.

If you're looking for your Rambo knife, I dropped it in a box
at the police station.

Who'd have thought we'd be able to afford such luxury?

Do you think we should get you a Camping Wife?

Have we got everything we need to be completely miserable
for three days in the Gower?

Hell of a second honeymoon.

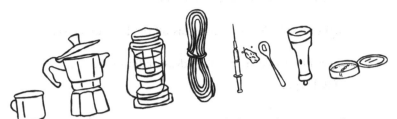

Don't forget the mini cricket set,
the Bluetooth speaker and the heroin.

. . . On Day One of Your Honeymoon

Oh, brilliant! There's loads of jigsaws here.

. . . About Other Men

We could ask your brother if he'd like to come swimming
with us.

. . . When You See His Internet Search History

You know those are not nice words, don't you?

I think it's time we built you a bunker.

Might be safer just to throw this off the back of a ferry.

You realise there's probably a desk dedicated to you at GCHQ . . .

Your Dark Web loyalty card must be nearly full.

I don't know how the porn industry would cope without you.

Is there anything in the shed I shouldn't allow to get warm?

Just be careful what hobby clubs you join.

Promise me you haven't left a manifesto on YouTube.

. . . While He's Buying Trainers

I know Gary's got a pair, but Gary is cool.

Get the ones that don't spoil with kebab juice on them.

Ooh, these are nice – nobody would ever guess how monstrous your feet are.

Have they got any that don't smell of bins after a month?

I think we'll find something more suitable in the Betterware catalogue.

Isn't this a bit of a young person's shop, darling?

Oh dear. Are you trying to keep up with Stormzy?

Do they have ones that make you walk straight after two drinks?

Not really your thing, style, is it?

. . . In an Expensive Restaurant

Two tables for one, please.

Don't worry about it being pricey – I've put three of your guitars on Ebay.

Why are we here? Have you been watching *Pretty Woman* again?

I'd never really thought through the possibility
that the kids would take after you.

It's lovely, this. It reminds me of when we were first going out and of absolutely no other point since.

You look nervous. Shall we get you some crayons?

Well, this is very nice. That's twice now.

Don't worry – I phoned ahead and they said it was alright for you to be here.

Tuck your shirt in. You look like you've been running away from the police.

The last time you took me somewhere this nice, I started reading your emails.

. . . When He's Telling You What Israel and Palestine Need to Do

Well, thank God you're here, it was all starting to get a bit out of hand.

With respect, you still haven't had the balls to prune next door's apple tree that's hanging into our garden.

If only the world had more harmless idiots like you in it, it would be so much more peaceful.

I see someone's heard the phrase 'two-state solution' today.

Are you being the Prime Minister again, darling?

... While You're Giving Birth to His Child

Well, thanks for everything. You can go now.

This is YOUR FAULT.

I've got an idea: you can have the next one.

If he looks a bit like your mate Chris, that's just your imagination, OK?

Are you off soon? Only the dad's coming in about half an hour.

I hope it doesn't look like you, because I never want to see your face again.

Next time, get someone else pregnant.

If it takes after you, there's always adoption.

☢ If you're feeling a bit useless at the moment, don't worry: you're useless all the time.

. . . When His Gym Membership Comes Up for Renewal

Have you actually been to the gym any time during the last three prime ministers?

You know Virgin Active isn't a charity, don't you?

Shall we just burn the money now?

You could be putting this towards a funeral plan.

. . . When You're Away for the Night

If you phone my room and someone else answers, it's just me doing an impression.

I've got a little surprise for you. Look in the cupboard under the stairs. I've put a new mop head on for you.

I just thought I'd say hello while Todd's having a shower.

Got a nice view of the basketball courts from here. Could you get my binoculars biked over?

I can't talk for long. There's an airline pilot staying here who's got a knot in his shoulder.

Can we afford for me to live here?

Can you dig out the fax machine there? I'm just trying to send some divorce stuff from the business centre.

How are the batteries doing on that Fleshlight?

Just so you know: the instruction manual for the Hoover's in the bottom drawer.

... When He Shaves His Beard Off

Well, that's taken years off our marriage.

Can I have your autograph?
I loved you in *Teletubbies*.

Shit. I'd forgotten about this guy.

. . . When He Falls for a Two-for-One Offer and Ends Up Coming Home with Too Many Mushrooms

Well, this is going to be a fun month.

If you think I'm drinking Mushroom Gin, you can bloody think again.

This is like the time you came home with three shoes.

Are you identifying as a forest floor now?

Are we opening a mushroom theme park?

If you make the 'fun-gi' joke, I will shove these in your eyes.

What's for dinner tonight, then?

Wrong house.

 Did someone give you these, or are you a fucking idiot?

. . . In the Afterglow

Not sure how many more times I can do this.

Do I have to be here for the next one?

Do you know what would look nice on that ceiling? A big picture of Tom Hardy.

Do you have to take an entrance exam to become a nun?

Seen a lot of *Carry On* films, have you?

There must be some other way we can do this.

Next time I could strap an iPad across your face and read a book while we're at it.

Would it help if you didn't have to climb the stairs first?

Did I miss something?

Hang on a minute – we don't *want* any more kids. We don't have to do this any more!

Look, this is just getting a bit stale now – shall we try kayaking instead?

I'm not sure what all the fuss is about. Are you?

Which religion is it that doesn't have to do this?

Might be worth giving ketamine a go.

We'll get there one day.

 That was like trying to kill a zombie.

...When He Starts Looking at a Smallholding in France

The world isn't asking for your recording studio.

Are you transitioning into a farmer?

...When He Gets Back from Therapy

Whose fault was it this week?

My God – you're a different man.

You didn't tie him up, did you?

What would be a really good gift
if I'd done something bad?

. . . When He's Putting Together His Fantasy Football Squad because Jack's Mate Won Ten Grand Last Year

Just to be clear, don't you dare talk to me about this in bed.

Good for you, babe. I'm so glad you've found a way to justify gambling with our money.

Aww, are you trying to make friends with the rough boys again?

Don't come crying to me when you get relegated and have to find new mates.

Don't forget to never update me about this at any point during the football season.

If there's one thing I've never thought when you are going on about football, it's 'there might be money in this'.

I think you're supposed to know things to play this game, darling.

Well, you better watch yourself, because I'm signing up to play Fantasy Husbands with the girls.

. . . When He's Dressed Up as a Murderer for Halloween

You know you're just dressed as yourself.

Oh look – you've come as your inner child.

But you wore this to my niece's christening.

It's supposed to be a bit of fun, not spark a manhunt.

You look a *little* bit too comfortable dressed like that.

I can feel a career change coming on.

I hate to say this, but it suits you.

You look like Worzel Gummidge accepting an MBE.

What did you murder? A bag of potatoes?

There's a big do at Broadmoor tonight – shall we drop you off there?

. . . When He's Banging on about How Worried He Is about His Brother's Marriage but Is Obviously Enjoying Watching It Fail

You were laughing about this in your sleep last night.

You should start a blog about this.

The main thing is: you've never let it get to you that you weren't his best man.

You know this isn't *Emmerdale*? You know this is real life?

I don't think I've seen you this happy since you saw that three-for-one offer on Punk IPA.

It's funny how your eyes sparkle when you talk about this.

What's all this about? Is it because he's got a better body than you?

It's funny, sibling rivalry: you think it's deep within you, but actually it's all over your face.

Is this because at the wedding he made you sit next to that pale cellist from Stroud?

I'll say one thing: your brother might be better than you in nearly every single way, but you are winning at wives.

Do you think you'll be this pleased when our marriage fails?

Is now a bad time to tell you I've always fancied him?

You know the reason they're splitting up is because he wouldn't shut up about his brother's marriage failing?

Poor Liam. Did Noel kick you out of his band again?

Hey, Cain – Abel's on the phone. He's just calling to gloat about the collapse of your marriage.

☢ Are they splitting up? I feel bad for sleeping with him now.

. . . When He's Telling the Guests How He 'Did' the Flooring

Yeah, I don't know what the guy on his hands and knees for three days would have done without your tea-making expertise.

It's amazing how you managed to do it with your hands on your hips.

Have you forgotten who you aren't?

Is this in the same way you 'did' the giving birth?

. . . When He Drives past the Motorway Turn-Off

Oh, OK, tree-killer, let's go the long way.

Well, this is getting one star on Tripadvisor.

I'm sensing some deep self-loathing right now. Would that be about right?

REMEMBER TO TAKE YOUR COAT OFF BEFORE YOU COME TO BED
Does this Count as making an effort?
Gone on Tinder. Back in a few days. xxx

I DON'T KNOW WHO YOU ARE BUT GET OUT OF MY HOUSE

IF YOU CAN'T FIND IT IT'S IN THE CHARITY SHOP

IF YOU'RE DRUNK THE ANSWER'S NO AS USUAL

IDEA: BE LESS OF A TWAT

. . . When He's Looking at Photos of Himself from Twenty Years Ago

That was that evening you smiled.

Well, it's not a time machine, but it'll have to do.

THAT'S what I saw in you!

I'm thinking of leaving you for this photograph.

Look away, darling. You'll only upset yourself.

It won't be long till you look like that again if you keep mainlining that kombucha.

How did I not notice that you were good-looking?

. . . When He Comes Home with Something from a Skip

Oh good. A big tin.

Are you identifying as a Womble now?

Hey – you know what we should get for all these things you keep bringing home? A skip.

Bad dog. In your bed!

Is this some sort of offering? How very sweet. Now go away.

If this is a romantic gesture you can pack your bags now.

Apparently George Clooney leaves Amal's favourite perfume on her dresser for her when he's been away. You might want to give that some thought.

. . . When He's Doing His Impressions

Can you do anyone who isn't a paedophile?

You should try and get on *New Faces 1988*.

All of these just sound like A Boring Man at the End of His Marriage.

You know Pontins do scholarships . . .

. . . When He's in a Bad Mood

Work's really stressing you out at the moment – why don't you go away for a few years?

It's somehow more watchable when the Hulk does this.

Well, at least we know your eyebrows still work.

We should bottle this atmosphere and sell it to the Taliban.

Looking forward to finding what I've done to not deserve this.

I, Cathy, take thee, Craig,
to be my wedded husband,
to have and to hold,
from this day forward,
for better, for worse,
for richer, for poorer,
in sickness and in health,
for laziness, for grumpiness,
and your lack of hygiene,
even when playing FIFA
for 3 days straight,
to love and to cherish,
'til death do us part.

Are you absolutely sure putting up with this was in the marriage vows?

This reminds me why I had that panic attack before we got married.

Someone from the British Sign Language Association just texted to ask if you can keep it down a bit.

Why don't you go in the cellar and just be with your bats for a while?

Have you had a poo today? You know what you're like when you haven't done your potty . . .

Oh! You're in a bad mood! I thought a Siberian winter had moved in.

Cheer up, love, I feel like I'm stuck in a Stephen King novel.

Here, could I borrow your face to freeze these salmon fillets?

Can you make a bit more noise, please? I'm worried someone on the International Space Station doesn't know exactly what you think of me.

Phone the Met Office! Hurricane Shitmouth is here!

MON	TUE	WED	THU	FRI	SAT	SUN
Gan - Doc			Get milk ✓			
				CHOKE THE CHICKEN		
		Yoga-11am				
					get birthday gift	

Don't be like this.

I had a wank planned for this evening.

I'm just going to quietly go back in time and not marry you.

Could you at least wear a bear suit when you're in this mood so I have something cute to look at?

Keep it down, love – we don't want Relate's helicopter hovering over the house again.

Oh good. It's the *EastEnders* re-enactment society. I'll put the kettle on.

I'm glad you're in this mood, actually – I'd forgotten where every single one of my nerve endings are.

Look, it's perfectly understandable that you're in this mood. After all, you are a colossal bellend.

Oh look – a giant toddler. Would you like some turkey dinosaurs?

. . . When He Says He's Going to Light the Barbecue

It is your time. Go. Send smoke signals to other local men. Your tribe must gather and burn sausages.

I wish you were this possessive about the washing.

DO NOT TOUCH! Professionals only

Do we know anybody who composes fanfares?

Don't forget to ask a grown-up to help you with this bit.

Look out, everyone. There's a sausage arsonist on the loose.

You know, I really should get better at announcing when *I'm* going to cook.

Just so you know, I've hidden the lighter fluid. We can't afford another fence.

Ah. Another sacrificial kebab offering to the gods.

Shall I have my heartburn tablets now?

Shall I put the oven on for when it goes wrong?

. . . When He's Looking at Second-Hand Motorbikes Online

Have you got a grant from the National Lottery?

. . . On Your Anniversary

Good news: I haven't forgotten our wedding anniversary. Bad news: that's your present.

. . . When He's Complaining about the Price of a Drink for the Fifteenth Time on Your Romantic Weekend Break in Gothenburg

Well, next year we'll go to Libya.

You've now complained about that one drink more times than we've been on romantic breaks.

This is such a lovely city for you to moan in.

What's Swedish for 'divorce lawyer'?

Oh, you've got the words 'romantic' and 'watchdog' mixed up again.

Did I change my name to Tripadvisor?

This is lovely. I never feel this uncomfortable at home.

If it'll shut you up, I'll buy the rest of the fucking drink off you.

Maybe you should just rent the next one.

The main thing is not to enjoy it.

Yeah, it is astonishing that drinks here aren't free, like they are in every other city in the world.

Well, thank God you've never spent £500 on a *Smokey and the Bandit* poster to hang in the shed.

. . . When He's Recounting His Golf Game to You

Please, God, make him stop.

Is this *you* talking or are you quoting Bruce Forsyth's autobiography?

I've got an idea: from now on, why don't you tell all your golf stories to the tank in the loft?

And how are the Freemasons?

Oh, I love your entitled white men stories.

Are you trying to guarantee that we don't have sex this month?

Wait there a minute, I'm going to go and get you Jimmy Tarbuck's phone number.

Of all the people you could aspire to be like, you choose Nick Faldo.

Do I look like Sue Barker? Well, shut up, then.

Do you think you could leave this story in the garage with your golf clubs?

Hold that thought, I'm just going to get some lube before my vagina seals itself up.

I was just telling Samantha today
how you invented curry.

. . . When You're in the Wrong

This is horrible, being wrong. Now I know what you feel like the rest of the time.

Well, I look forward to hearing about this every fucking day for the rest of my life.

. . . When He's Trying Not to Sound like He Fancies Someone Who He's Now Mentioned Fifteen Times a Day for the Last Three Weeks

If I had a pound for every time you've mentioned them this week, we could afford a divorce.

Doing anything nice for your one-month anniversary?

How fascinating. Do, please, tell me less.

Are you being paid to advertise this person?

Oh good. This again. It's been nine minutes since the last nail in my heart.

It must be so hard for you two, being apart like this.

Shall I get you some new aftershave?

Oh dear, someone's ears must be burning. I do hope their whole head doesn't explode in flames.

Shall we get you a signed poster?

... When He's about to Get the Snip

Why don't we go for the Ken from Barbie look and get the whole thing removed?

... When He Buys a Pair of UGG Slippers

Did you kill a car salesman and cut up his coat?

... When He Suggests Renewing Your Wedding Vows

If we're going to do that, I'm going to renew my hen weekend first.

... When He's Doing One of the Two Days of Gardening He'll Do All Year

Fancy a cup of tea, Alan Shitmarsh?

Your knees just texted me to say they're going to need the ambulance at about half four. Look, darling, you don't have to tunnel out – just leave.

Are you digging this plot for you or me?

. . . On Holiday

This honestly couldn't be any more perfect. Except if I was on my own.

I suppose you're going to be dressing like Imran Khan for two weeks.

That lethal-looking stretch of water might be worth a swim in.

I need some cream on my back, so just for now, I'm lifting the touching ban.

What day do you want to have the shits this time?

All this daytime drinking is making me forget what you're like to live with.

Who are you going on holiday with next year?

Quick. Let's get a photo taken while we don't look like we hate each other.

Are you going to use some sun cream this year, or try and beat the sun again?

That book must be good. You haven't moaned about the heat for two hours.

God, I miss everyone else.

Remember to leave *some* of the buffet for the other 300 guests.

That tan really brings out the red in your eyes.

You smile so much more when you're on holiday. See if you can remember how to do it when we get home.

Don't try your French on that waiter again tonight. He looked like he was going to burst.

Why don't you get a massage while I can actually see who's doing it?

Tell you what: it's a lot harder to ignore each other when there's no one else around.

 I've heard the sharks round here are vegetarian. Why don't you go for a swim?

. . . In a Greetings Card

Nice to have met you.

I don't want to give you the wrong idea, so I'll just leave it at this.

I wrote you a poem. You'll find it scratched into the table.

I know you really go in for Valentine's Day, so I'd just like to say Happy Birthday for whenever that is (I can't remember) and Merry Christmas and I'm sorry for your loss xxx

. . . When He's Trying to Turn the Cupboard under the Stairs into a Microbrewery

Is brewing beer a good idea for someone who hasn't got the patience to peel open bacon packaging?

I'm not sure you can make a double dry-hopped New England IPA from a kit you got at Wilko.

How many hipster Ewoks do you think you'll be serving on a Friday?

I knew I shouldn't have bought you that book about Victorian poisoners.

And this is definitely nothing to do with Al-Qaeda?

. . . When He's Off to the Football

Shall I pick you up in an ambulance, or do you want to call it yourself?

. . . At the Top of the Eiffel Tower

Unconventional place for a break-up, but here we go . . .

This is where I asked Phil to marry me. Wonder what he's doing now.

I thought I'd feel something up here, but . . . nothing.

There's something I've always wanted to say to you. That sound you make when you're chewing really gets on my tits.

Doesn't the financial district look beautiful?

You know this was only meant to be temporary, don't you? A bit like us.

Darling, look! There's a bloke down there going through the bins.

I still say Blackpool's better.

Weird to think this'll be here long after we've both remarried.

. . . While You're Going through Your Wedding Photographs

It's funny – I don't remember any of this.

Christ. It's amazing what booze'll help you get through.

Actually, your face doesn't look as bad as I remember.

Look at you. Gorgeous. You were the hottest guy I'd ever kissed at that point.

Have we still got the receipt for all this?

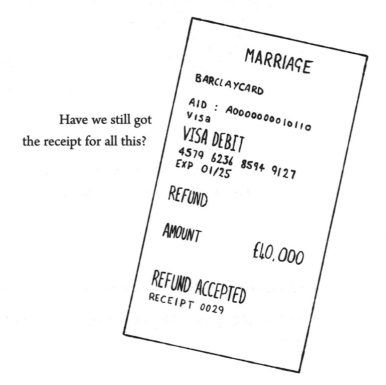

I can still remember when your dad went down on one knee and begged me to take you off his hands.

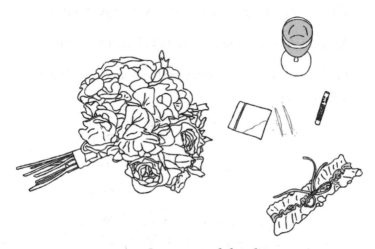

I was so tired that day.
If it wasn't for the coke your nan gave me,
I don't know if I'd have got through it.

I still follow that pageboy on Facebook. He's a big lad now.

Your dad said I'd grow to like you. Just shows you what he knows.

. . . While He's on the Phone to Someone

(MOUTHING SILENTLY) I'm leaving you.

. . . When He's Explaining Why the Way Eric Cantona Used to Play Was More like Ballet than Football and How He Was a Postmodern Analogy of the Emerging Redrawing of the Lines around Masculinity

Those skirting boards need a lick of paint.

. . . Ever

☢ Do you reckon we could split this house down the middle?

☢ What is it you do again?

☢ Darling, have we still got those cyanide pills?

☢ How do you want to play it if you end up in a wheelchair?

☢ I've got it. I know who you remind me of: gangrene.

☢ I'm going to miss this when we're not together any more.

☢ I was talking to a really interesting divorce lawyer the other day.

☢ Don't forget to sign my guestbook before you leave this relationship.

☢ Right, well, that's my life done. What else can you ruin?

☢ I'm just nipping out to get my 'No Regrets' tattoo removed.

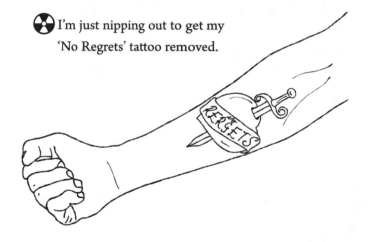

☢ Tell you who's a good husband . . .

If you have been offended by anything in this book, please fill in this complaints form and send it to the publisher directly.

I/we/they (delete as applicable) bought this book in the expectation that it would make me/us/them laugh.

However, when I/we/they read out some of the lines from it to my/our/their husband/wife/partner, they/they/they left me/us/them and ran off with a dentist/local councillor/labrador, and are now living happily in Toulouse/Cleethorpes/sin.

I/we/they demand that you apologise/refund me/unpublish this book immediately, or you will leave me/us/them no alternative but to seek legal advice/knock over your bins/go off-grid and become a cress farmer.

I/we/they look forward to your grovelling/legalistic/arsey reply.

Yours furiously,

Here is the reply you will receive.

Dear Sir/Madam/neither,

Thank you for submitting your complaint. We would kindly refer you to the title of the book.

Yours Sincerely,

Chief Replier

Department of Complaints

Hachette Books